T0208732

Are You Ready To Endure?

John Marini

WESTBOW
PRESS®
A DIVISION OF THOMAS NELSON
& ZONDERVAN

WestBow Press books may be ordered through booksellers or by contacting:

WestBow Press
A Division of Thomas Nelson & Zondervan
1663 Liberty Drive
Bloomington, IN 47403
www.westbowpress.com
1 (866) 928-1240

ISBN: 978-1-9736-5434-6 (sc)
ISBN: 978-1-9736-5435-3 (e)

Library of Congress Control Number: 2019901945

Print information available on the last page.

WestBow Press rev. date: 03/15/2019

Preface

I was always taught that the church will be raptured out before the tribulation. However, after years of studying God's Word my belief on this has changed. I pursued wisdom by asking the Holy Spirit to teach me the truth and to help me understand His Word. The purpose of this book is to share with you what I learned about how Jesus is coming back and what He said about it. Please pray for the Holy Spirit to reveal to you the Truth in God's Word.

Jesus said in John 14:26 (NKJV)

But the Helper, <u>the Holy Spirit</u>, whom the Father will send in My name, He will teach you all things, and bring to your remembrance all things that I said to you.

He also said in John 16:7-15 (NKJV)

*[7] Nevertheless I tell you the truth. It is to your advantage that I go away; for if I do not go away, <u>the Helper</u> will not come to you; but if I depart, <u>I will send Him to you</u>. .... [13] However, <u>when He, the Spirit of truth, has come,</u> **He will guide you into all truth**; for <u>He will not speak on His own authority, but whatever He hears He will speak; and He will tell you things to come.</u> [14] <u>He will glorify Me, for He will take of what is Mine and declare it to you.</u> [15] All things that the Father has are Mine. Therefore, I said that He will take of Mine and declare it to you.*

1 John 2:20, 21, 27

[20] But <u>you have an anointing from the Holy One, and you know all things</u>. [21] I have not written to you because you do not know the truth, but because you know it, and that no lie is of the truth……. [27] But <u>the anointing which you have received from Him abides in you, and you do not need that anyone teach you;</u> but as <u>the same anointing teaches you concerning all things, and is true, and is not a lie, and just as it has taught you, you will abide in Him</u>.

Contents

** All words of Jesus are in italics

Chapter 1

New Covenant with Israel

In this chapter, you will see how the nation of Israel came about and the covenants God made with them.

Genesis 32:28 (NKJV)

[28] And He said, "Your name shall no longer be called Jacob, but Israel; for you have struggled with God and with men, and have prevailed."

God changed Jacob's name to Israel. He had twelve sons, which became the twelve tribes of Israel -- God's people. God makes a covenant with His people, which is the law. This is our Old Testament.

Exodus 34:27-28 (NIV)

[27] Then the Lord said to Moses, "Write down these words, for in accordance with these words I have made a covenant with you and with Israel." [28] Moses was there with the Lord forty days and forty nights without eating bread or drinking water. And he wrote on the tablets the words of the covenant - the Ten Commandments.

Since man could not follow the commandments of the law perfectly, God had to make a new covenant with Israel.

A Messiah was needed, God gave four hundred prophesies about His coming. One of them is in chapter 9 of the book of Daniel, God spoke to Daniel about the coming of the Messiah (Jesus).

Daniel 9:24 (NKJV)

[24] "Seventy weeks are determined
For your people and for your holy city,
(The Messiah, Jesus will do the following)
To finish the transgression,
To make an end of sins,
To make reconciliation for iniquity,
To bring in everlasting righteousness,
To seal up vision and prophecy,
And to anoint the Most Holy.

These were fulfilled by Jesus; the New Testament or covenant was given to Israel by Him.

Jeremiah 31:31-34 (NKJV)

[31] "Behold, the days are coming, says the Lord, when I will make a **new covenant** with the house of Israel and with the house of Judah— [32] not according to the covenant that I made with their fathers in the day *that* I took them by the hand to lead them out of the land of Egypt, my covenant which they broke, though I was a husband to them, says the Lord. [33] But this *is* the covenant that I will make with the house of Israel after those days, says the Lord: I will put My law in their minds, and write it on their hearts; and I will be their God, and they shall be

<u>My people</u>. ³⁴No more shall every man teach his neighbor, and every man his brother, saying, 'Know the Lord,' for they all shall know Me, from the least of them to the greatest of them, says the Lord. For I will forgive their iniquity, and their sin I will remember no more."

Matthew 26:26-29, also in Mark 14:22-25, Luke 22:19-20, 1 Corinthians 11:23-26 (NKJV)

Jesus Institutes the Lord's Supper

²⁶ And as they were eating, Jesus took bread, blessed and broke *it,* and gave *it* to the disciples and said, *"Take, eat; this is My body."*

²⁷ Then He took the cup, and gave thanks, and gave *it* to them, saying, *"Drink from it, all of you.* ²⁸ <u>*For this is My blood of the* **new covenant**</u>*, which is shed for many for the remission of sins.* ²⁹ *But I say to you, I will not drink of this fruit of the vine from now on until that day when I drink it new with you in My Father's kingdom."*

Jesus came to bring salvation to everyone in the world.

John 3:16-17 (NKJV)

¹⁶ For God so loved <u>the world</u> that He gave His only begotten Son, that whoever believes in Him should not perish but have everlasting life.¹⁷ For God did not send His Son into the world to condemn the world, but that <u>the world through Him might be saved.</u>

He reached out to Israel first, giving them the first opportunity to receive salvation through Jesus Christ.

In Matthew 15:24 (NKJV) Jesus said,

²⁴ But He answered and said, *"I was not sent except to the **lost sheep of the house of Israel.**"*

Matthew 10:5-6 (NKJV)

Sending Out the Twelve

⁵ These twelve Jesus sent out and commanded them, saying: *"Do not go into the way of the Gentiles, and do not enter a city of the Samaritans.⁶ But go rather to the **lost sheep of the house of Israel.** So, we see that Israel was the first to hear about Jesus. Let's look at them being the first fruits.

The following is the definition of first fruit:
The first gathering of a season's produce. The first outcome, results, or rewards of anything.

Revelation 14:1-5 (NKJV)

The Lamb and the 144,000

¹ Then I looked, and behold, a Lamb standing on Mount Zion, and with Him one hundred *and* forty-four thousand, having His Father's name written on their foreheads. ² And I heard a voice from heaven, like the voice of many waters, and like the voice of loud thunder. And I heard the sound of harpists playing their harps. ³ They sang as it were a new song before the throne, before the four living creatures, and the elders; and no

one could learn that song except the hundred *and* forty-four thousand <u>who were redeemed from the earth</u>. ⁴ These are the ones who were not defiled with women, for they are virgins. These are the ones who follow the Lamb wherever He goes. <u>These were redeemed from *among* men, *being* **firstfruits** to God and to the Lamb</u>. ⁵ And in their mouth was found no deceit, for they are without fault before the throne of God.

In James 1:1 (NKJV), he opens with a greeting to the **Twelve Tribes**.

¹ James, a bondservant of God and of the Lord Jesus Christ,

<u>To the **twelve tribes** which are scattered abroad</u>

In the same chapter in verse 18, he makes an analogy that Israel is a firstfruit.

¹⁸ Of His own will He brought us forth by the word of truth, <u>that **we** might be a kind of **firstfruits** of His creatures</u>.

In the book of Acts, we see thousands of Jews being saved from chapters 1 to 9. Then in chapter 10, Peter gets a vision from God. This is where Cornelius and his family were the first gentiles to become part of this new covenant. This was the start of salvation being offered to **all** mankind.

Romans 1:16 (NKJV)

16 For I am not ashamed of the gospel of Christ, for it is the power of God to <u>salvation for everyone who believes,</u> <u>for the Jew first</u> and also for the Greek.

Romans 2:9-10 (NIV)

9 There will be trouble and distress for every human being who does evil: first for the Jew, then for the Gentile; 10 but glory, honor and peace for everyone who does good: <u>first for the Jew,</u> then for the Gentile.

So, there was a remnant from Israel that believed in Christ, which were the first fruits of the new covenant. (The remnant of Israel - Joel 2:32, Isaiah 10:20-23 and the first fruits - James 1:18, Revelation 14:4 (NKJV))

Chapter 2

God's Wrath Is Never Upon His People

Jesus came the first time to redeem us from our sins, so that we can have eternal life with Him in heaven. According to the Book of Revelation, God will pour out His wrath on the ungodly, before His second coming when He will bring judgement. We as believers in Christ <u>will not</u> experience God's wrath during this time.

Hebrews 9:28 (NKJV)

²⁸ so Christ was offered once to bear the sins of many. <u>To those who eagerly wait for Him He will</u> **appear** a **second time**, apart from sin, for salvation.

In the end times, God will have wrath on the ungodly men and women.

Wrath (meaning - extreme or violent rage, an act in vengeance or punishment) is what non-believers or ungodly people will experience.

1 Thessalonians 5:1-11 (NKJV)

The Day of the Lord

¹ But concerning the times and the seasons, brethren, you have no need that I should write to you. ² For you yourselves know

perfectly that <u>the **day** of the Lord so comes as a thief in the night</u>. ³ For when they say, "Peace and safety!" then sudden destruction comes upon them, as labor pains upon a pregnant woman. And they shall not escape. ⁴ But you, brethren, are not in darkness, so that <u>this Day should overtake you as a thief</u>. ⁵ You are all sons of light and sons of the day. We are not of the night nor of darkness. ⁶ Therefore let us not sleep, as others *do,* but let us <u>watch and be sober</u>. ⁷ For those who sleep, sleep at night, and those who get drunk are drunk at night. ⁸ But let us who are of the day be sober, putting on the breastplate of faith and love, and *as* a helmet the hope of salvation. ⁹ **For God did not appoint us to wrath**, but to obtain salvation through our Lord Jesus Christ, ¹⁰ who died for us, that whether we wake or sleep, we should live together with Him. ¹¹ Therefore comfort each other and edify one another, just as you also are doing.

2 Peter 2:9 (NKJV)

⁹ *then* the Lord **knows how to deliver the godly** (righteous) <u>out of temptations</u> **and** to reserve the unjust under punishment for <u>the day of judgment</u>,

Let's look at how God protected His people through His wrath in the Old Testament. In chapters 6 and 7 of the book of Genesis, Noah and his family were protected from the rain and flood by the ark, only the ungodly perished. Also, chapters 7 – 11 in Exodus, you can see that the plagues were God's wrath on Pharaoh and the people in Egypt. None of these plagues came upon Israel, His people. In chapters 8 and 9 of Ezekiel, even when some of the people of Israel were doing abominations (any detestable act or practice) against God, He sent death angels to kill them. His wrath was upon the people who were doing the abominations. He protected the righteous by sending first an angel with an ink horn, to put a mark on the foreheads of the righteous ones. Then the death angels were sent out. They were commanded **not** to kill the righteous that had the <u>mark of God on their foreheads</u>.

God's wrath (plagues) will be on all the people who have not yet received Jesus as their Lord and Savior. However, He is still reaching out to them because God did not make hell for mankind, but for Satan and the fallen angels.

Matthew 25:41 (NKJV)

[41] "Then He will also say to those on the left hand, 'Depart from Me, you cursed, into the <u>everlasting fire</u> **prepared for the devil and his angels**:

As you can see from the next two verses, God loves everyone and wants us all to be with Him in heaven.

1 Timothy 2:3-4 (NKJV)

[3] For this *is* good and acceptable in the sight of God our Savior, [4] <u>who desires **all** men to be saved and to come to the knowledge of the truth.</u>

2 Peter 3:9 (NKJV)

[9] The Lord is not slack concerning *His* promise, as some count slackness, but is longsuffering toward us, <u>not willing that **any** should perish but that **all** should come to repentance.</u>

In the following scriptures, God is giving those who haven't received Christ yet one last chance to do so, before He comes for the final judgement.

Revelation 15:1 (NKJV)

Prelude to the Bowl Judgments {God's anger upon those who disobey Him in the form of plagues} figurative.

¹ Then I saw another sign in heaven, great and marvelous: <u>seven angels having the seven last **plagues**, for in them the **wrath of God** is complete.</u>

Seven bowls (plagues) are coming upon those who have not received Jesus as their Lord and Savior.

Based on the Fourth and Fifth Bowl, men still did not repent from their sins and turn their lives to Christ.

Revelation 16:8-11 (NKJV)

The Fourth Bowl: Men Are Scorched

⁸ Then the fourth angel poured out his bowl on the sun, and power was given to him to scorch men with fire. ⁹ And men were scorched with great heat, and they blasphemed the name of God who has power over these plagues; and <u>they **did not repent (those who have rejected Christ)** and give Him glory.</u>

Fifth Bowl: Darkness and Pain

[10] Then the fifth angel poured out his bowl on the throne of the beast, and his kingdom became full of darkness; and they gnawed their tongues because of the pain. [11] They blasphemed the God of heaven because of their pains and their sores and **did not repent** of their deeds.

The next set of scriptures show that even though God's heart and desire is for **all** men to be saved, not **all** men will choose Christ.

Revelation 22:14-15 (NKJV)

[14] Blessed *are* those who do His commandments, that they may have the right to the tree of life and may enter through the gates into the city (heaven).

[15] But **outside** (people who are to burn in hell) *are* dogs and sorcerers and sexually immoral and murderers and idolaters, and whoever loves and practices a lie.

1 Corinthians 6:9-10 (NKJV)

[9] Do you not know that the unrighteous will not inherit the kingdom of God? Do not be deceived. Neither fornicators, nor idolaters, nor adulterers, nor homosexuals, nor sodomites, [10] nor thieves, nor covetous, nor drunkards, nor revilers, nor extortioners will inherit the kingdom of God.

** If you have not received Jesus as your Lord and Savior, please stop now and pray this prayer.

Lord Jesus, I admit that I am a sinner and in need of your forgiveness. I believe that you died on the cross to forgive my sins. I ask you now to come into my heart and be the Lord of my life. Help me to know you better and fill me with your Holy Spirit, who is my helper. Please guide me to a church where I can grow and learn more about you. In Jesus Name, Amen.

Chapter 3

Saints Are Sealed and Protected

As we just read in the previous chapter, God had put a mark on the righteous ones to protect them. In the same manor, we, as God's people, will be protected when God's wrath (plagues) comes on the ungodly because we are sealed with the Holy Spirit.

Jesus was sealed first by the Father.

John 6:26-27 (NKJV)

²⁶Jesus answered them and said, *"Most assuredly, I say to you, you seek Me, not because you saw the signs, but because you ate of the loaves and were filled. ²⁷Do not labor for the food which perishes, but for the food which endures to everlasting life, which the Son of Man will give you, because <u>God the Father has **set His seal on Him**</u>."* (seal – meaning the Holy Spirit on Jesus)

Now to all who become children of God through Christ.

2 Corinthians 1:20-22 (NKJV)

²⁰For all the promises of God in Him *are* Yes, and in Him Amen, to the glory of God through us. ²¹Now He who establishes us with you in Christ and has anointed us *is* God, ²²<u>who also has **sealed us**</u> and <u>given us **the Spirit in our hearts as a guarantee**</u>.

Ephesians 1:13-14 (NIV)

[13] And you also were included in Christ when you heard the message of truth, the gospel of your salvation. When you believed, <u>you were marked in him with a seal, the promised Holy Spirit,</u> [14]<u>who is a deposit guaranteeing our inheritance</u> until the redemption of those who are God's possession—to the praise of his glory.

Ephesians 4:30 (NKJV)

[30] And do not grieve <u>the Holy Spirit of God, by whom **you were sealed** for the **day** of redemption.</u>

Note: This is why Satan doesn't want us to know about the Holy Spirit, for the Spirit will keep us strong through all that is coming upon the earth, He is our guarantee of eternal life.

In one of John's visions in the book of Revelation, he saw those that were sealed, the 144,000----12,000 from each tribe. Then he saw a multitude, which is all believers.

Revelation 7:1-14 (NKJV)

The Sealed of Israel

[1] After these things I saw four angels standing at the four corners of the earth, holding the four winds of the earth, that the wind should not blow on the earth, on the sea, or on any tree. [2] Then I saw another angel ascending from the east, **having the seal of the living God**. And he cried with a loud voice to the four angels to whom it was granted to harm the

earth and the sea, ³ saying, "**Do not** harm the earth, the sea, or the trees **till we have sealed the servants of our God on their foreheads**." ⁴ And I heard the **number of those who were sealed**. One hundred *and* forty-four thousand of all the tribes of the children of Israel *were* sealed:

⁵ of the tribe of Judah twelve thousand *were* sealed;
of the tribe of Reuben twelve thousand *were* sealed;
of the tribe of Gad twelve thousand *were* sealed;
⁶ of the tribe of Asher twelve thousand *were* sealed;
of the tribe of Naphtali twelve thousand *were* sealed;
of the tribe of Manasseh twelve thousand *were* sealed;
⁷ of the tribe of Simeon twelve thousand *were* sealed;
of the tribe of Levi twelve thousand *were* sealed;
of the tribe of Issachar twelve thousand *were* sealed;
⁸ of the tribe of Zebulun twelve thousand *were* sealed;
of the tribe of Joseph twelve thousand *were* sealed;
of the tribe of Benjamin twelve thousand *were* sealed.

⁹ After these things I looked, and behold, a great multitude which no one could number, of all nations, tribes, peoples, and tongues, standing before the throne and before the Lamb, clothed with white robes, with palm branches in their hands, ¹⁰ and crying out with a loud voice, saying, "Salvation *belongs* to our God who sits on the throne, and to the Lamb!" ¹¹ All the angels stood around the throne and the elders and the four living creatures, and fell on their faces before the throne and worshiped God, ¹² saying:

"Amen! Blessing and glory and wisdom,
Thanksgiving and honor and power and might,
Be to our God forever and ever.
Amen."

¹³ Then one of the elders answered, saying to me, "Who are these arrayed in white robes, and where did they come from?" (talking about the multitude, for John knew the tribes of Israel)

¹⁴ And I said to him, "Sir, you know."

So, he said to me, "These are the ones who come out of the great tribulation and washed their robes and made them white in the blood of the Lamb.

In the following scriptures, God commands the demonic angels not to harm any of the believers.

Revelation 9:3-5 [fifth trumpet] (NKJV)

³ Then out of the smoke locusts came upon the earth. And to them was given power, as the scorpions of the earth have power. ⁴ They were **commanded not** to harm the grass of the earth, or any green thing, or any tree, but only **those men who do NOT have the seal of God on their foreheads**. ⁵ And they were not given *authority* to kill them (ungodly), but to torment them *for* five months. Their torment *was* like the torment of a scorpion when it strikes a man.

Chapter 4

Tribulation

Jesus said that we will have tribulation in our lives, yet our faith in Him will carry us through whatever we may experience. Jesus gives us the hope we need. When we seek Him through these times, He gives us direction and peace through it all.

Tribulation (meaning--condition of affliction and distress) is what the believers go through because of Christ in us and our belief in Him.

John 16:33 (NKJV)

*³³ These things I have spoken to you, that in Me you may have peace. In the world you will have tribulation; but **be of good cheer**, I have overcome the world.*"

Acts 14:21-22 (NKJV)

²¹ And when they had preached the gospel to that city and made many disciples, they returned to Lystra, Iconium, and Antioch, ²² strengthening the souls of the disciples, exhorting them to continue in the faith, and saying, "We must through many tribulations enter the kingdom of God."

1 Thessalonians 3:1-4 (NKJV)

¹ Therefore, when we could no longer endure it, we thought it good to be left in Athens alone, ² and sent Timothy, our brother and minister of God, and our fellow laborer in the gospel of Christ, to establish you and encourage you concerning your faith, ³ that no one should be shaken by these afflictions; for you yourselves know that we are appointed to this. ⁴ For, in fact, we told you before when we were with you that we would suffer tribulation, just as it happened, and you know.

Revelation 1:9 (NKJV)

⁹ I, John, both your brother and companion in the tribulation and kingdom and patience of Jesus Christ, was on the island that is called Patmos for the word of God and for the testimony of Jesus Christ.

Romans 5:1-5 (NKJV)

¹ Therefore, having been justified by faith, we have peace with God through our Lord Jesus Christ, ² through whom also we have access by faith into this grace in which we stand, and rejoice in hope of the glory of God. ³ And not only that, but we also glory in tribulations, knowing that tribulation produces perseverance; ⁴ and perseverance, character; and character, hope. ⁵ Now hope does not disappoint, because the love of God has been poured out in our hearts by the Holy Spirit who was given to us.

Jesus also spoke about a great tribulation.

Matthew 24:17-21, also in Mark 13:19 (NKJV)

17 Let him who is on the housetop not go down to take anything out of his house. 18 And let him who is in the field not go back to get his clothes. 19 But woe to those who are pregnant and to those who are nursing babies in those days! 20 And pray that your flight (act of fleeing or escaping from danger) *may not be in winter or on the Sabbath. 21 <u>For then there will be great tribulation, such as has not been since the beginning of the world until this time, no, nor ever shall be.</u>*

Jesus <u>said He will</u> **shorten** the **tribulation period** <u>for the</u> **elect sake** (all believers).

Matthew 24:22, also in Mark 13:20 (NKJV)

*22 And unless those days were shortened, <u>no flesh would be saved</u>; but for the **elect's sake** those **<u>days will be shortened</u>**.*

Jesus said after this tribulation, then we will see Him.

Matthew 24:29-31, also in Mark 13:24-27, Luke 21:25-28 (NKJV)

*29 "**Immediately <u>after the tribulation</u>** of those days the sun will be darkened, and the moon will not give its light; the stars will fall from heaven, and the powers of the heavens will be shaken. 30 **<u>Then the sign of the Son of Man will appear in heaven, and then all the tribes of the earth will mourn, and they will see the Son of Man</u>***

coming on the clouds of heaven with power and great glory. [31] _And He will send His angels with a great sound of a trumpet, and they will gather together His elect from the four winds, from one end of heaven to the other._

Chapter 5

Patience of the Saints During the Tribulation Period

Saint - meaning a believer in Christ.

Persecution will be more intense before Jesus returns. We need to have a close relationship with Jesus and the support of one another for strength and encouragement. When you go through rough times, it is always good to have someone there to help you.

Ecclesiastes 4:9-10 (NKJV)

⁹ Two *are* better than one,
Because they have a good reward for their labor.
¹⁰ For if they fall, <u>one will lift up his companion.</u>
But woe to him *who is* alone when he falls,
For *he has* no one to help him up.

Hebrews 10:24-25 (NKJV)

²⁴ And let us consider one another <u>in order to stir up love and good works,</u> ²⁵ <u>not forsaking the assembling of ourselves together,</u> as *is* the manner of some, but exhorting *one another,* and <u>so much the more as you see the Day approaching.</u>

Luke 21:28 (NKJV)

"Now when these things begin to happen, look up and lift up your heads, because your redemption draws near."

Revelation 13:7-10 [beast and dragon] (NKJV)

[7] It was granted to him (the anti-christ) to make **war with the saints** and to overcome them. And authority was given him over every tribe, tongue, and nation. [8] All who dwell on the earth will worship him, whose names have **not** been written in the Book of Life of the Lamb slain from the foundation of the world.

[9] If anyone has an ear, let him hear. [10] He who leads into captivity shall go into captivity; he who kills with the sword must be killed with the sword. **Here is the patience and the faith of the saints.**

Revelation 14:9-12 (NKJV)

[9] Then a third angel followed them, saying with a loud voice, "If anyone worships the beast and his image, and receives *his* mark on his forehead or on his hand, [10] he himself shall also drink of the wine of the wrath of God, which is poured out full strength into the cup of His indignation. He shall be tormented with fire and brimstone in the presence of the holy angels and in the presence of the Lamb. [11] And the smoke of their torment ascends forever and ever; and they have no rest day or night, who worship the beast and his image, and whoever receives the mark of his name." [12] **Here is the patience of the saints;**

here *are* **those who keep the commandments of God and the faith of Jesus.**

*Note that the church, which are the saints, are still here on earth.

Chapter 6

Called to Stand Firm to The End

Standing firm is the evidence that a person is truly committed to Jesus. The power of the Holy Spirit helps us to endure through anything we may be experiencing.

2 Thessalonians 3:3-5 (NKJV)

³ But the Lord is faithful, <u>who will establish you and guard *you* from the evil one</u>. ⁴ And we have confidence in the Lord concerning you, both that you do and will do the things we command you. ⁵ <u>Now may the Lord direct your hearts into the love of God and into the patience of Christ.</u>

Hebrews 3:14 (NKJV)

¹⁴ For we have become partakers of Christ if <u>we **hold** the beginning of our confidence steadfast **to the end**</u>.

Hebrews 6:11 (NKJV)

¹¹ And we desire that each one of <u>you show the same diligence to the full assurance of hope **until the end**</u>.

Hebrews 10:25 (NKJV)

²⁵ not forsaking the assembling of ourselves together, as *is* the manner of some, but exhorting *one another*, and so much the more <u>as you see the **Day** approaching</u>.

James 5:7-8 (NKJV)

⁷ Therefore be patient, brethren, <u>until the coming of the Lord</u>. See *how* the farmer waits for the precious fruit of the earth, waiting patiently for it until it receives the early and latter rain. ⁸ You also be patient. **Establish your hearts,** <u>for the coming of the Lord is at hand</u>.

1 Peter 1:3-7 (NKJV)

³ Blessed *be* the God and Father of our Lord Jesus Christ, who according to His abundant mercy has begotten us again to a living hope through the resurrection of Jesus Christ from the dead, ⁴ <u>to an inheritance</u> incorruptible and undefiled and that does not fade away, reserved in heaven for you, ⁵ **who are kept by the power of God through faith** for salvation ready <u>to be revealed in the last time.</u>

⁶ In this you greatly rejoice, though now for a little while, if need be, you have been grieved by various trials, ⁷ that the genuineness of your faith, *being* much more precious than gold that perishes, though it is tested by fire, **may be found** to praise, honor, and glory <u>at the revelation of Jesus Christ,</u>

1 Timothy 6:12-15 (NIV)

¹²Fight the good fight of the faith. <u>Take hold of the eternal life</u> to which you were called......I charge you ¹⁴<u>to keep this command</u> without spot or blame <u>until the appearing of our Lord Jesus Christ</u>, ¹⁵which God will bring about in his own time—God, the blessed and only Ruler, the King of kings and Lord of lords,

2 Timothy 4:8 (NIV)

⁸Now there is in store for me the crown of righteousness, which the Lord, the righteous Judge, will award to me <u>on that day</u>—and not only to me, but also to all who have <u>longed for his appearing.</u>

1 John 2:28 (NKJV)

²⁸And now, little children, **abide in Him,** <u>that when He appears</u>, we may have confidence and not <u>be ashamed before Him at His coming</u>.

1 John 3:2 (NKJV)

²Beloved, now we are children of God; and it has not yet been revealed what we shall be, but <u>we know that when **He is revealed**</u>, we shall be like Him, for we shall see Him as He is.

Revelation 2:25-26 (NKJV)

25 But hold fast what you have till I come. 26 And he who overcomes, and keeps My works until the end, to him I will give power over the nations—

Matthew 24:13-14 (NKJV)

13 But he who endures to the end shall be saved. 14 And this gospel of the kingdom will be preached in all the world as a witness to all the nations, and then the end will come.

Matthew 10:22, also in Mark 13:13 (NKJV)

22 And you will be hated by all for My name's sake. But he who endures to the end will be saved.

If you do not endure in your faith, you will be counted among the ungodly. Our salvation does not give us freedom to do whatever we want. Do not be fooled by the saying, "once saved always saved". Do your thoughts and actions reflect Christ?

Chapter 7

Jesus Will Be with Us to the End

Knowing that Jesus will never leave or forsake us, enables us to live a life of stability in our faith. We can go to Him for courage and trust Him to get us through, no matter what we face in life. God loves us too much to leave us the way we are. He is always helping us to become more loving, kind, peaceful, longsuffering, patient, faithful, gentle and self-controlled, just like Jesus Himself.

2 Timothy 4:18 (NKJV)

¹⁸ And <u>the Lord</u> will deliver me from every evil work <u>and preserve *me* for His heavenly kingdom.</u> To Him *be* glory forever and ever. Amen!

Psalm 121:7-8 (NKJV)

⁷ <u>The Lord shall preserve you from all evil</u>;
He shall preserve <u>your soul</u>.
⁸ <u>The Lord shall preserve</u> your going out and your coming in
From this time forth, and even forevermore.

Matthew 28:19-20 (NKJV)

¹⁹ Go therefore and make disciples of all the nations, baptizing them in the name of the Father and of the Son and of the Holy

Spirit, ²⁰ teaching them to observe all things that I have commanded you; and lo, I am with you always, even to the end of the age." Amen.

The power of the Holy Spirit has been given to us to keep us strong on our journey through life.

John 14:15-17 (NKJV)

Jesus Promises Another Helper

¹⁵ "If you love Me, keep My commandments. ¹⁶ And I will pray the Father, and He will give you another Helper, that He may abide with you forever— ¹⁷ the Spirit of truth, whom the world cannot receive, because it neither sees Him nor knows Him; but you know Him, for He dwells **with** you and will be **in** you.

1 Corinthians 1:4-8 (NIV)

⁴ I always thank my God for you because of his grace given you in Christ Jesus. ⁵ For in him you have been enriched in every way— with all kinds of speech and with all knowledge— ⁶ God thus confirming our testimony about Christ among you. ⁷ Therefore you do not lack any spiritual gift as you eagerly wait for our Lord Jesus Christ to be revealed. ⁸ **He will** also keep you **firm** to the **end,** so that you will be blameless on the day of our Lord Jesus Christ.

1 Thessalonians 3:11-13 (NKJV)

¹¹ Now may our God and Father Himself, and our Lord Jesus Christ, direct our way to you. ¹² And may the Lord make you

increase and abound in love to one another and to all, just as we *do* to you, [13] so that **He** may **establish your hearts blameless in holiness** before our God and Father **at the coming of our Lord Jesus Christ** with **all** His saints.

Philippians 1:3-6 (NKJV)

[3] I thank my God upon every remembrance of you, [4] always in every prayer of mine making request for you all with joy, [5] for your fellowship in the gospel from the first day until now, [6] being confident of this very thing, that **He** who has begun a good work in you will complete *it* **until the day of Jesus Christ;**

Colossians 3:4 (NKJV)

[4] When Christ *who is* our life appears, then you also will appear with Him in glory.

1 Thessalonians 5:23 (NKJV)

[23] Now may the **God of peace Himself** sanctify you completely; and may your whole spirit, soul, and body be preserved blameless at the coming of our Lord Jesus Christ.

Chapter 8

How Jesus Is Coming

We hear so many opinions on how and when Jesus is coming back. In this chapter and the following six chapters, the scriptures make it clear about what Jesus Himself said about His coming and the events that will happen at that time.

First, we must believe that He is coming.

Hebrews 9:28 (NKJV)

²⁸ so Christ was offered once to bear the sins of many. <u>To those who eagerly wait for Him He will</u> **appear** a **second time**, apart from sin, for salvation.

He is coming in the clouds.

Acts 1:9-11 (NKJV)

Jesus Ascends to Heaven

⁹ Now when He had spoken these things, while they watched, He was taken up, and <u>a cloud received Him out of their sight</u>. ¹⁰ And while they looked steadfastly toward heaven as He went up, behold, two men stood by them in white apparel, ¹¹ who also said, "Men of Galilee, why do you stand gazing up into heaven? <u>This *same* Jesus, who was taken up from</u>

you into heaven, will so come in **like manner** as you saw Him go into heaven."

Matthew 26:64, also in Mark 14:62 (NKJV)

[64]Jesus said to him, *"It is as you said. Nevertheless, I say to you, hereafter you will <u>see the Son of Man sitting at the right hand of the Power and coming on the clouds of heaven."</u>*

He is coming with His angels.

Matthew 16:27-28, also in Mark 8:38, 9:1, Luke 9:27 (NKJV)

[27] *For the <u>Son of Man will come in the glory of His Father with His angels</u>, and <u>then He will reward each according to his works</u>.* [28] *"Assuredly, I say to you, there are <u>some standing here who shall not taste death till they see the Son of Man coming in His kingdom."</u>*

Matthew 25:31 (NKJV)

[31] *"<u>When the Son of Man comes in His glory, and all the holy angels with Him</u>....*

2 Thessalonians 1:7 (NKJV)

[7] and to *give* you who are troubled rest with us <u>when the Lord Jesus is revealed from heaven with His mighty angels,</u>

Chapter 9

Jesus Comes as A Thief

Notice when you are reading the next set of scriptures, when Jesus was talking about coming as a thief, he was not referring to someone who steals, but as one who is taking all the believers away at <u>an unexpected hour</u>. As the scripture below states, **no one, not even Jesus** or the angels **know the time** God will appoint for His Son to return to earth. For us to be prepared for His coming, we must either continue, or start to develop a close relationship with Jesus our Lord and Savior. This will enable us to have the power and strength we will need to endure to the end.

Matthew 24:36-51 (NKJV)

*36 "<u>But of that **day** and **hour no one knows**, not even the angels of heaven</u>, but My Father only. 37 But as the days of Noah were, so also will the coming of the Son of Man be. 38 For as in the days before the flood, they were eating and drinking, marrying and giving in marriage, until the day that Noah entered the ark, 39 and did not know until the flood came and took them all away, so also will the coming of the Son of Man be. 40 Then two men will be in the field: one will be taken and the other left. 41 Two women will be grinding at the mill: one will be taken and the other left. 42 <u>Watch therefore, for you **do not know what hour** your Lord is coming</u>. 43 <u>But know this, that if the master of the house **had known what hour the thief would come**</u>, he would have watched and not allowed his house to* *be broken into. ⁴⁴ Therefore you also <u>be ready, for the Son of Man is</u>* *<u>coming at an </u>**<u>hour you do not expect</u>**.*

Mark 13:32-37 (NKJV)

No One Knows the Day or Hour

³² "But of that day and <u>hour no one knows, not even the angels</u> *<u>in heaven, nor the Son,</u> but only the Father. ³³ Take heed, watch* *and pray; for you do not know when the time is. ³⁴ It is like a man* *going to a far country, who left his house and gave authority to his* *servants, and to each his work, and commanded the doorkeeper to* *watch. ³⁵ Watch therefore, <u>for you do not know when the master of</u>* *<u>the house is coming</u>—in the evening, at midnight, at the crowing of* *the rooster, or in the morning— ³⁶ lest, coming suddenly, he find you* *sleeping. ³⁷ And what I say to you, I say to all: Watch!"*

Luke 12:35-40 (NKJV)

The Faithful Servant and the Evil Servant

³⁵ "Let your waist be girded and your lamps burning; ³⁶ and you *yourselves be like men who wait for their master, when he will* *return from the wedding, that when he comes and knocks they may* *open to him immediately. ³⁷ Blessed are those servants whom the* *master, when he comes, will find watching. Assuredly, I say to you* *that he will gird himself and have them sit down to eat and will come* *and serve them.³⁸ And if he should come in the second watch, or come* *in the third watch, and find them so, blessed are those servants. ³⁹ But* *know this, that if the <u>master of the house had known </u>**<u>what hour</u>** <u>the</u>* ***<u>thief</u>** <u>would come,</u> he would have watched and not allowed his house*

to be broken into. *⁴⁰ Therefore you also <u>be ready, for the</u>* **<u>Son of Man</u>** **<u>is coming at an hour you do not expect</u>**.*"*

Revelation 16:15 (NKJV)

¹⁵ "Behold, <u>I am coming as a thief</u>. Blessed is he who watches, and keeps his garments, lest he walk naked and they see his shame."

1 Thessalonians 5:1-4 (NKJV)

The Day of the Lord

¹ But concerning the times and the seasons, brethren, you have no need that I should write to you. ² For you yourselves know perfectly <u>that the</u> **day** <u>of the Lord so</u> **comes as a thief in the** **night**…. ⁴ But you, brethren, are not in darkness, so that <u>this</u> **day** <u>should</u> **overtake you** <u>as a thief</u>.

2 Peter 3:10-13 (NIV)

¹⁰ But the **day** of the Lord will **come like a thief**. The heavens will disappear with a roar; the elements will be destroyed by fire, and the earth and everything done in it will be laid bare.

¹¹ Since everything will be destroyed in this way, what kind of people ought you to be? You ought to live holy and godly lives ¹² as you look forward to the day of God and speed its coming. That day will bring about the destruction of the heavens by fire, and the elements will melt in the heat. ¹³ But in keeping with his promise we are looking forward to a new heaven and a new earth, where righteousness dwells.

Chapter 10

Every Eye Will See Jesus At His Coming

When Christ comes, everyone will see Him including believers and non-believers. There will be a loud trumpet sound, a shout, and an angel speaking that will be heard over the entire earth. This will be a joyful event for those who have received Him as their personal Lord and Savior. I will speak in a later chapter what will happen to those who reject Christ.

1 Thessalonians 4:16 (NKJV)

[16] For the Lord Himself will descend from heaven <u>with a shout</u>, <u>with the</u> <u>voice of an archangel</u>, and <u>with the trumpet of God</u>. And the dead in Christ will rise first.

A similar event happened when God revealed Himself to Israel at Mount Sinai, it was very loud, so loud that the people were afraid.

Exodus 19:16 (NKJV)

[16] Then it came to pass on the third day, in the morning, that there were thunderings and lightnings, and a thick cloud on the mountain; and the <u>sound of the trumpet was very loud</u>, so that all the people who *were* in the camp trembled.

The people were afraid of God's presence.

Exodus 20:18 (NKJV)

¹⁸Now all the people witnessed the thunderings, the lightning flashes, <u>the sound of the trumpet, and the mountain smoking; and when the people saw *it*, they trembled and</u> stood afar off.

Revelation 1:7 (NKJV)

⁷Behold, <u>He is coming with clouds,</u> and **every eye will see Him**, even they who pierced Him. And all the tribes of the earth will mourn because of Him. Even so, Amen.

Luke 17:24 (NKJV)

²⁴ For as the lightning that flashes out of one part under heaven shines to the other part under heaven, so also the Son of Man will be in His day.

When lightning flashes every eye in its path sees it.

Luke 21:20, 25-28 (NKJV)

*²⁰ "But when you see Jerusalem surrounded by armies, then know that its desolation is near....... ²⁵ "And there will be signs in the sun, in the moon, and in the stars; and on the earth distress of **nations**, with perplexity, the sea and the waves roaring; ²⁶ men's hearts failing them from fear and the expectation of those things which are coming on the earth, for the powers of the heavens will be shaken. ²⁷ <u>Then they will see the Son of Man coming in a cloud with power and great glory. ²⁸ Now when these things begin to happen, look up and lift up your heads, because your redemption draws near.*"</u>

Chapter 11

Jesus Will Raise Us Up on The Last Day

Jesus said four times in the book of John, that He will raise us up at the last day. Last day meaning – there are no more days after that day. For if there was one day after, then it wouldn't be the last.

John 6:39,40,44,47,48,53,54 (NIV)

*³⁹ And this is the will of him who sent me, that I shall lose none of all those he has given me, but <u>raise them up at the last day</u>. ⁴⁰ For my Father's will is that everyone who looks to the Son and believes in him shall have eternal life, **and I will raise them up at the last day**......*

*Jesus answered. ⁴⁴ "No one can come to me unless the Father who sent me draws them, <u>and I will raise them up</u> **at the last day**...... ⁴⁷ Very truly I tell you, the one who believes has eternal life. ⁴⁸ I am the bread of life...........*

*⁵³ Jesus said to them, "Very truly I tell you, unless you eat the flesh of the Son of Man and drink his blood, you have no life in you. ⁵⁴ Whoever eats my flesh and drinks my blood has eternal life, and <u>I will raise them up</u> **at the last day**.*

The Jews must have also believed in the resurrection because Martha spoke to Jesus concerning her brother Lazarus when he was in the tomb.

John 11:21-24 (NKJV)

²¹ Now Martha said to Jesus, "Lord, if You had been here, my brother would not have died. ²² But even now I know that whatever You ask of God, God will give You."

²³ Jesus said to her, *"Your brother will rise again."*

²⁴ Martha said to Him, "I know that he <u>will rise again in the resurrection</u> **at the last day**."

Chapter 12

We Will Meet Jesus In the Air

This is the day all believers in Jesus have been waiting for. In heaven there will be no more pain and suffering. We will experience peace, joy and love like we have never known before. We will be with Him forever!

The dead in Christ will rise first.

1 Thessalonians 4:15-17 (NKJV)

[15] For this we say to you by the word of the Lord, that <u>we who are **alive** *and* **remain** until the coming of the Lord will by no means precede those who are asleep</u> (dead). [16] For the Lord Himself will descend from heaven with a shout, with the voice of an archangel, and with the trumpet of God. And <u>the dead in Christ will rise first.</u> [17] **Then we who are alive *and* remain** <u>shall be caught up together with them in the clouds to meet the Lord in the air.</u> And <u>thus we shall **always** be with the Lord.</u>

John 5:25-29 (NKJV)

[25] *Most assuredly, I say to you, the hour is coming, and now is, when <u>the dead will hear the voice</u> of the Son of God; and those who hear will live.* [26] *For as the Father has life in Himself, so He has granted the Son to have life in Himself,* [27] *and has given Him authority to execute judgment also, because He is the Son of Man.* [28] *Do not*

marvel at this; for the hour is coming in which all who are in the graves <u>will hear His voice</u> [29] <u>and come forth</u>—those who have done good, to the resurrection of life, and those who have done evil, to the resurrection of condemnation.

Daniel 12:1b-2 (NKJV)

Prophecy of the End Time

[1b] ......And at that time your people shall be delivered,
Everyone who is found written in the book.
[2] And many of those who sleep in the dust of the earth shall awake,
<u>Some to everlasting life,</u>
<u>Some to shame *and* everlasting contempt.</u>

According to Paul's teaching in Corinthians, this event will happen suddenly.

1 Corinthians 15:35-52 (NIV)

The Resurrection Body

[35] But someone will ask, "How are the dead raised? With what kind of body will they come?" [36] How foolish! What you sow does not come to life unless it dies. [37] When you sow, you do not plant the body that will be, but just a seed, perhaps of wheat or of something else. [38] But God gives it a body as he has determined, and to each kind of seed he gives its own body. [39] Not all flesh is the same: People have one kind of flesh, animals have another, birds another and fish another. [40] There

are also heavenly bodies and there are earthly bodies; but the splendor of the heavenly bodies is one kind, and the splendor of the earthly bodies is another. [41] The sun has one kind of splendor, the moon another and the stars another; and star differs from star in splendor.

[42] So will it be with the resurrection of the dead. The body that is sown is perishable, it is raised imperishable; [43] it is sown in dishonor, it is raised in glory; it is sown in weakness, it is raised in power; [44] it is sown a natural body, it is raised a spiritual body.

If there is a natural body, there is also a spiritual body. [45] So it is written: "The first man Adam became a living being"; the last Adam, (referring to Jesus) a life-giving spirit. [46] The spiritual did not come first, but the natural, and after that the spiritual. [47] The first man was of the dust of the earth; the second man is of heaven. [48] As was the earthly man, so are those who are of the earth; and as is the heavenly man, so also are those who are of heaven. [49] And just as we have borne the image of the earthly man, so shall we bear the image of the heavenly man.

[50] I declare to you, brothers and sisters, that flesh and blood cannot inherit the kingdom of God, nor does the perishable inherit the imperishable. [51] Listen, I tell you a mystery: We will not all sleep, but we will all be changed— [52] in a flash, in the twinkling of an eye, at the last trumpet. For the trumpet will sound, the dead will be raised imperishable, and we will be changed.

Chapter 13

Jesus Sends His Angels to Separate the Righteous from the Ungodly

Angels are messengers of God, which He uses throughout the Bible to accomplish what He wants to be done here on earth. They will be sent to reap the harvest and separate the believers from the non-believers.

Matthew 13:24-30 (NKJV)

The Parable of the Wheat and the Tares

²⁴ Another parable He put forth to them, saying: *"The kingdom of heaven is like a man who sowed good seed in his field;* ²⁵ *but while men slept, his enemy came and sowed tares among the wheat and went his way.* ²⁶ *But when the grain had sprouted and produced a crop, then the tares also appeared.* ²⁷ *So the servants of the owner came and said to him, 'Sir, did you not sow good seed in your field? How then does it have tares?'* ²⁸ *He said to them, 'An enemy has done this.' The servants said to him, 'Do you want us then to go and gather them up?'* ²⁹ *But he said, 'No, lest while you gather up the tares you also uproot the wheat with them.* ³⁰ Let both grow together until the harvest, and at the time of harvest I will say to the reapers, "First gather together the tares and bind them in bundles to burn them but gather the wheat into my barn."*

Matthew 13:36-43 (NKJV)

The Parable of the Tares Explained

36 Then Jesus sent the multitude away and went into the house. And His disciples came to Him, saying, "Explain to us the parable of the tares of the field."

37 He answered and said to them: *"He who sows the good seed is the Son of Man.* 38 *The field is the world, the good seeds are the sons of the kingdom, but the tares are the sons of the wicked one.* 39 *The enemy who sowed them is the devil, the <u>harvest is the **end of the age**</u>, and the reapers are the angels.* 40 *Therefore as the tares are gathered and burned in the fire, so it will be at the end of this age.* 41 *The <u>Son of Man will **send out His angels**, and they will gather out of His kingdom all things that offend, and those who practice lawlessness,</u>* 42 *<u>and will cast them into the furnace of fire</u>. There will be wailing and gnashing of teeth.* 43 *Then the righteous will shine forth as the sun in the kingdom of their Father. He who has ears to hear, let him hear!*

Matthew 13:47-50 (NKJV)

The Parable of the Dragnet

47 *"Again, the kingdom of heaven is like a dragnet that was cast into the sea and gathered some of every kind,* 48 *which, when it was full, they drew to shore; and they sat down and gathered the good into vessels but threw the bad away.* 49 *So <u>it will be at **the end of the age**. <u>The **angels will come forth**, **separate the wicked from among the just**,</u>* 50 *<u>and cast them into the furnace of fire</u>. There will be wailing and gnashing of teeth."*

As you can see from the verses above, those who refuse to turn their lives over to Christ, will suffer eternal consequences.

Chapter 14

Jesus Will Bring Forth Judgement

Some people believe that there will be a second chance to receive Christ after the rapture. In my studies however, I found this to be incorrect. Why, you ask? Because the following scriptures prove that <u>judgement will happen</u> **at His coming**.

2 Timothy 4:1 (NKJV)

¹ I charge *you* therefore before God and the Lord Jesus Christ, <u>who will judge the living and the dead</u> **at His appearing** and His kingdom:

Matthew 24:45-51 Also in Luke 12:42-46 (NKJV)

⁴⁵ *"Who then is a faithful and wise servant, whom his master made ruler over his household, to give them food in due season? ⁴⁶ Blessed is that servant whom his master, <u>when he comes,</u> will find so doing.⁴⁷ Assuredly, I say to you that he will make him ruler over all his goods.⁴⁸ But if that evil servant says in his heart, 'My master is delaying his coming,' ⁴⁹ and begins to beat his fellow servants, and to eat and drink with the drunkards, ⁵⁰ <u>the master of that servant will come</u> on a day when he is not looking for him and at an hour that he is not aware of,⁵¹ <u>and will cut him in two and appoint him his portion with the hypocrites.</u> There shall be weeping and gnashing of teeth.*

Matthew 25:31-34, 41-46 (NKJV)

[31] "<u>When the Son of Man comes in His glory</u>, and all the holy angels with Him, <u>then He will sit on the throne of His glory</u>. [32] <u>All the nations will be gathered before Him</u>, and <u>He will separate them one from another</u>, as a shepherd divides his sheep from the goats. [33] And He will set the sheep on His right hand, but the goats on the left. [34] Then the King will say to those on His right hand, 'Come, you blessed of My Father, inherit the kingdom prepared for you from the foundation of the world: ....

[41] "Then He will also say to those on the left hand, '<u>Depart from Me, you cursed, into the everlasting fire prepared for the devil and his angels.</u>[42] for I was hungry and you gave Me no food; I was thirsty and you gave Me no drink; [43] I was a stranger and you did not take Me in, naked and you did not clothe Me, sick and in prison and you did not visit Me.'

[44] "Then they also will answer Him, saying, 'Lord, when did we see You hungry or thirsty or a stranger or naked or sick or in prison, and did not minister to You?' [45] Then He will answer them, saying, 'Assuredly, I say to you, inasmuch as you did not do it to one of the least of these, you did not do it to Me.' [46] <u>And these will go away into everlasting punishment, but the righteous into eternal life.</u>"

John 12:48 (Living Bible)

[48] But all who reject Me and My message will be judged at the Day of Judgment by the truths I have spoken.

2 Thessalonians 1:6-10 (NKJV)

⁶since *it is* a righteous thing with God to repay with tribulation those who trouble you, ⁷and to *give* you who are troubled rest with us when the Lord Jesus is revealed from heaven with His mighty angels, ⁸in flaming fire taking vengeance on those who do not know God, and on those who do not obey the gospel of our Lord Jesus Christ. ⁹These shall be punished with everlasting destruction from the presence of the Lord and from the glory of His power, ¹⁰when He comes, in that Day, to be glorified in His saints and to be admired among all those who believe, because our testimony among you was believed.

Revelation 20:11-15 (NKJV)

The Great White Throne Judgment

¹¹Then I saw a great white throne and Him who sat on it, from whose face the earth and the heaven fled away. And there was found no place for them. ¹²And I saw the dead, small and great, standing before God, and books were opened. And another book was opened, which is *the Book* of Life. And the dead were judged according to their works, by the things which were written in the books. ¹³The sea gave up the dead who were in it, and Death and Hades delivered up the dead who were in them. And they were judged, each one according to his works. ¹⁴Then Death and Hades were cast into the lake of fire. This is the second death. ¹⁵And anyone not found written in the Book of Life was cast into the lake of fire.

Daniel 12:1-2 (NKJV)

Prophecy of the End Time

[1] "At that time Michael (the archangel) shall stand up,
The great prince who stands *watch* over the sons of your people;
And there shall be a time of trouble,
Such as never was since there was a nation,
Even to that time.
And at that time your people shall be delivered,
Everyone who is found written in the book. (Book of Life)
[2] And many of those who sleep in the dust of the earth shall awake,
Some to everlasting life,
Some to shame *and* everlasting contempt.

2 Corinthians 6:2 (NKJV)

[2] For He says: "In an acceptable time I have heard you,
And in the day of salvation I have helped you."
Behold, now *is* the accepted time; behold, now *is the day of salvation.

Hebrews 3:7-15 (NKJV)

Be Faithful

[7] Therefore, as the Holy Spirit says:
"**Today,** if you will hear His voice,

[8]Do not harden your hearts as in the rebellion,
In the day of trial in the wilderness,
[9]Where your fathers tested Me, tried Me,
And saw My works forty years.
[10]Therefore I was angry with that generation,
And said, 'They always go astray in *their* heart,
And they have not known My ways.'
[11]So I swore in My wrath,
'They shall not enter My rest.'"

[12]Beware, brethren, lest there be in any of you an evil heart of unbelief in departing from the living God; [13]but exhort one another daily, while it is called "Today," lest any of you be hardened through the deceitfulness of sin. [14]For we have become partakers of Christ **if we hold the beginning of our confidence steadfast to the end**, [15]while it is said:

"Today, if you will hear His voice,
Do not harden your hearts as in the rebellion."

We will not be saved by the things we do, but by our faith in Christ and the finished work that He did on the cross. We need to repent, turn away from our sins and live a righteous life. We can do this through the power of Christ as we allow Him to reign in our hearts. Those who refuse to repent and turn to Christ will suffer eternal consequences. Hell is a real place.

Galatians 2:16 (NKJV)

[16]knowing that a man is not justified by the works of the law but by faith in Jesus Christ, even we have believed in Christ Jesus, that we might be justified by faith in Christ and not by

53

the works of the law; <u>for by the works of the law no flesh shall be **justified**</u>.

Revelation 22:12-21 (NKJV)

[12] <u>*"And behold, I am coming quickly, and My reward is with Me, to give to everyone according to his work.*</u> [13] *I am the Alpha and the Omega, the Beginning and the End, the First and the Last."*

Chapter 15

Get to Know Who You Are in Christ

As a believer in Jesus Christ, knowing who we are in Him, is the basis of our existence. We must grow in the knowledge of who God says we are, because of what Jesus did on the cross. As we learn what the Lord says about us, this will transform our lives. We will know the truth which sets us free. Jesus died so we could have eternal life. He gave us everything to live in victory in this world. When lies or deception come, we will be able to stand against those ways of thinking by renewing our minds to the truth in God's Word.

Revelation 22:7, 14-16 (NKJV)

[7] *"Behold, I am coming quickly! Blessed is he who keeps the words of the prophecy of this book."* .....

[14] Blessed *are* those who do His commandments, that they may have the right to the tree of life and may enter through the gates into the city. [15] But outside *are* dogs and sorcerers and sexually immoral and murderers and idolaters, and whoever loves and practices a lie.

[16] *"I, Jesus, have sent My angel to testify to you these things in the churches. I am the Root and the Offspring of David, the Bright and Morning Star."*

When people join the army, navy, or marines, etc., they are taught to survive in battle by learning how to use their weapons. We are in the army of God, so we need to prepare ourselves for spiritual battle. Get to know who you are in Christ (Christ meaning anointed one) and the weapons that we have in Him.

2 Corinthians 10:3-6 (NKJV)

[3] For though we walk in the flesh, we do not war according to the flesh. [4] For the weapons of our warfare *are* not carnal but mighty in God for pulling down strongholds, [5] casting down arguments and every high thing that exalts itself against the knowledge of God, bringing every thought into captivity to the obedience of Christ, [6] and being ready to punish all disobedience when your obedience is fulfilled.

We need to endure and stand firm in our belief. (as noted in chapters 5 and 8)

The way to stand is to be grounded in the Word of God. Jesus, the Holy Spirit and the Father will sustain us and keep us strong through these times. Remember, He said He will **never** leave us or forsake us.

Supernatural strength will come from the Holy Spirit.

Ephesians 6:10-18 (NKJV)

The Whole Armor of God

[10] Finally, my brethren, **be strong in the Lord** and in the **power of His** might. [11] Put on the whole armor of God, that you may

be able to stand against the wiles of the devil. [12] For we do not wrestle against flesh and blood, but against principalities, against powers, against the rulers of the darkness of this age, against spiritual *hosts* of wickedness in the heavenly *places*. [13] Therefore take up the whole armor of God, <u>that you may be able to withstand in the evil day, and having done all, to stand.</u>

[14] Stand therefore, having girded your waist with truth, having put on the breastplate of righteousness, [15] and having shod your feet with the preparation of the gospel of peace; [16] above all, taking the shield of faith with which, you will be able to quench all the fiery darts of the wicked one. [17] And take the helmet of salvation, and the sword of the Spirit, which is the word of God; [18] **praying always** with all prayer and supplication in the Spirit, <u>being watchful</u> <u>to this end</u> with all perseverance and supplication for all the saints.

To be strengthened spiritually and to know God's power within you, pray the following prayers for yourself and others.

2 Thessalonians 1:11-12 (NKJV)

[11] Therefore we also **<u>pray always</u>** <u>for you that our God would count you worthy of *this* calling</u> and fulfill all the good pleasure of *His* goodness and <u>the work of</u> **<u>faith with power</u>**, [12] that the name of our Lord Jesus Christ may be glorified in you, and you in Him, according to the grace of our God and the Lord Jesus Christ.

Colossians 1:9-14 (NKJV)

⁹ For this reason we also, since the day we heard it, do not cease to **pray** for you, and to ask that you may be filled with the knowledge of His will in all wisdom and spiritual understanding; ¹⁰ that you may walk worthy of the Lord, fully pleasing *Him*, being fruitful in every good work and increasing in the knowledge of God; ¹¹ **strengthened** with all might, according to **His glorious power**, for all patience and longsuffering with joy; ¹² giving thanks to the Father who has qualified us to be partakers of the inheritance of the saints in the light. ¹³ He has delivered us from the power of darkness and conveyed *us* into the kingdom of the Son of His love, ¹⁴ in whom we have redemption through His blood, the forgiveness of sins.

Ephesians 1:15-21 (NKJV)

Prayer for Spiritual Wisdom

¹⁵ Therefore I also, after I heard of your faith in the Lord Jesus and your love for all the saints, ¹⁶ do not cease to give thanks for you, making mention of you in my prayers: ¹⁷ that the God of our Lord Jesus Christ, the Father of glory, may give to you the spirit of wisdom and revelation in the knowledge of Him, ¹⁸ the eyes of your understanding being enlightened; that you may know what is the hope of His calling, what are the riches of the glory of His inheritance in the saints, ¹⁹ and what *is* the exceeding greatness of **His power** toward us who believe, according to the working of **His mighty power** ²⁰ which He worked in Christ when He raised Him from the dead and seated *Him* at His right hand in the heavenly *places,* ²¹ far above all principality and power and might and dominion, and every

name that is named, not only in this age but also in that which is to come.

Ephesians 3:16-21 (NIV)

A Prayer for the Ephesians

[16] **I pray** that out of His glorious riches He may <u>strengthen you with power through His Spirit</u> in your inner being, [17] so that Christ <u>may dwell in your hearts through faith</u>. And I pray that you, <u>being rooted and established in love,</u> [18] <u>may have power,</u> together with all the Lord's holy people, to grasp how wide and long and high and deep is the love of Christ, [19] and to know this love that surpasses knowledge - that you may be filled to the measure of all the fullness of God.

[20] Now to him who is able to do immeasurably more than all we ask or imagine, <u>according to his power</u> that is at work within us, [21] to him be glory in the church and in Christ Jesus throughout all generations, for ever and ever! Amen.

The revealing of the anti-christ.

Judas Iscariot betrayed Jesus when Satan entered him.

Luke 22:3 (NKJV)

[3] Then <u>Satan entered Judas,</u> <u>surnamed Iscariot,</u> who was numbered among the twelve.

John 17:12 (NKJV)

*12 While I was with them in the world, I kept them in Your name. Those whom You gave Me I have kept; and none of them is lost except the **son of perdition** (Judas), that the Scripture might be fulfilled.*

In the same way, Satan will enter the anti-christ in the end times.

2 Thessalonians 2:3,9-10 (NKJV)

3 Let no one deceive you by any means; for *that Day will not come* unless the falling away comes first, and the man of sin is revealed, the **son of perdition**,......9 The coming of the *lawless one* is according to the working of Satan, with all power, signs, and lying wonders, 10 and with all unrighteous deception among those who perish, because they did not receive the love of the truth, that they might be saved.

When Satan entered Judas (Luke 22:3, John 13 :27), Jesus was heavily persecuted. In the same manor, when the man of sin (the anti-christ) is revealed (2 Thessalonians 2:3-6, 9-10), the body of Christ will experience heavy persecution. (This is what Jesus talked about in Matthew 24:17-21, also in Mark 13:19)

2 Timothy 3:1-5 (NKJV)

Perilous Times and Perilous Men

1 But know this, that in the last days perilous times will come: 2 For men will be lovers of themselves, lovers of money, boasters, proud, blasphemers, disobedient to parents, unthankful, unholy, 3 unloving, unforgiving, slanderers, without

self-control, brutal, despisers of good, ⁴ traitors, headstrong, haughty, lovers of pleasure rather than lovers of God, ⁵ having a form of godliness but denying its power. And from such people turn away!

We can receive His strength during this time by:

1. Reading and meditating on God's Word daily.
2. Praying and spending time with Him.
3. Trusting in His promises.
4. Staying connected with other believers.

According to James 5:11, those who **endure, will be blessed.** The Lord is full of compassion and mercy. Our reward will be living eternally with Jesus forever!

So, are "YOU" ready to endure?

Notes

Notes

Notes

Notes

Notes

Notes

Notes

Notes

Printed in the United States
By Bookmasters